The Piano Tuner

The Piano TUNER

Robert Astle

Cover design by Terry Gallagher/Doowah Design.
Cover photo of Robert Astle by Maria Antonella Pelizzari.

This book was printed on Ancient Forest Friendly paper.
Printed and bound in Canada by AGMV Marquis Imprimeur.

We acknowledge the support of The Canada Council for the Arts and the Manitoba Arts Council for our publishing program.

National Library of Canada Cataloguing in Publication

Astle, Robert
The piano tuner / Robert Astle.

(Performance series (Winnipeg, Man.))
ISBN 0-921833-95-4 (pbk.)

I. Title. II. Series.

PS8551.S875P43 2004 C812'.54
C2004-901788-8

Signature Editions www.signature-editions.com
P.O. Box 206, RPO Corydon, Winnipeg, Manitoba, R3M 3S7

For Guy Reber
1934–1982

storyteller
soldier
hockey player
ladies' man

E G B D F

Every Good Boy Deserves a Father

The Piano Tuner was first performed at the Centaur Theatre's Wildside Festival in Montreal, Quebec, January 9-17, 2003.

Written and performed by Robert Astle

Dramaturgy: Paul Lefebvre

Assistant: Mindy Parfitt

Original musical score and sound design: Henry Kucharzyk

Puppet design and construction: Almüt Ellinghaus-Mirbt

Scenic painting: Marina Popova

Lighting design: Michael Brunet

Video: Maria Antonella Pelizzari

Piano wrangler: Rachel Johnstone

Actor wrangler and videographer: David Gow

Photography: Maria Antonella Pelizzari, Pierro Hirsch

Running time: 71 minutes (no intermission)

THE PIANO TUNER

An outrageous dialogue between a piano tuner and a prepared piano.

Central Character:

Bob the Tuner. 50 years old, blind, wears sunglasses and a rumpled old linen suit.

Performance Note:

If possible, the entire performance should be done "blind," i.e. with eyes closed.

Reading Notes:

Various parts of the upright piano are mentioned in the descriptions of action.

Fall or fall board: The name given to the lid that covers the keys of a piano.

Top door, top board or scroll board: The removable top panel of an upright piano's case above the keyboard.

PART 1

THE PIANO FULL OF REGRETS

Lights come up on the stage, empty save for a derelict upright piano and a piano stool. Upstage of the piano is a canvas backdrop hung from the rafters. The stage seems to be set up for a concert.

We hear an announcement crackle out over the PA system:

Voice: Ladies and gentlemen, there is a problem with the piano and the concert will be delayed while the piano is retuned. You may turn on all your cellphones, pagers, and everything else that beeps. Call your loved ones, babysitters, accountants, lawyers, girlfriends, boyfriends, wives, lovers, real estate agents, stockbrokers. Feel free to buy and sell, book airline tickets, and order a pizza to go. If you must have a conversation, please keep your voices down. The direction of the hall regrets the delay, and wishes you a wonderful concert.

Scene 1: The Piano Full of Regrets

A blind piano tuner, Bob, is ushered into the space. He searches for the piano with his white cane. When he finds the piano, he taps it, giving the "trois coups" which signals the beginning.

All lights should focus within a small area near the piano. Lights come up to a slightly higher level, but the mood in the room should remain shadowy and hazy. The house lights should come down imperceptibly.

Bob gets down to work. He opens his tool case and places the tools on the top of the piano. Rather nervously, he addresses the public directly.

Bob: Evening, folks. This may take some time, but I'll be outta here before you can say John Jacob Jingle-Heimer-Schmitt.

If you wanna stay in the hall, I'd appreciate that you don't make too much noise and I promise you'll be rewarded by witnessing the miracle of piano tuning.

Bob hits the tuning fork and listens to the note sound. He opens the fall board covering the keys… He touches one key, but there is no sound. He checks the next key, then the next, and the next, and the next. He checks all the keys…not one sound.

Bob: *(Incredulously.)* Well I'll be a…son of a bitch… I got called to come here. They told me on the phone — it was an emergency — a broken string. And wouldn't ya know it, it's totally and completely dead — like someone tore the guts out of it. This is no emergency; I'm much too late. What we need here is a piano funeral, or just take it to the piano morgue! Sorry, folks, but there's nothing to be done.

He closes the piano, and tapping on the floor with his cane, struggles to find the exit. There is the sound of a very faint piece of music. Bob stops dead in his tracks. He returns to the instrument, reluctantly, but becoming more interested as the piano bursts forth with comical little segments of music.

Bob: Hello. Hello?

What the…?

Wait a second…

Just a darned…

Jesus… Hello? Anybody there?

Okay, you shitty upright…

If it wasn't for my…

Goddamned curiosity...

I'd be outta here by now.

Bob opens the fall board once again, and frantically follows the sound with his hands, trying to determine its source. He discovers something jammed in the keys...

Bob: Ahh-haaa, I knew there was something wonky here... Jesus, no wonder. Look at this, look at this. A ring! Y'know, a piano is a great place to find stuff...coins, pens, pencils, photos, credit cards, bottles...and rings. What can I tell ya? It's one of the greatest places for hiding stuff and losing stuff.

I once found a diamond ring in a piano. It was a Heintzman baby grand I was tuning for this woman. I was checking the keys and there was a definite clicking sound under F–1. Anyways, when I cleaned under the key, I found a ring. After I finished the tuning, the woman came home... Y'know, when I showed her the ring, shit, if she didn't break into tears. It was like seeing that ring filled her with such despair. I thought maybe I shouldn'ta showed her the damn ring. She seemed kinda fragile, and I helped her to sit on the piano bench. After she calmed down a little she told me that thirty years before, she'd had a terrible fight with her best girlfriend, because she thought her friend had stolen her ring — she was furious, because it was a diamond ring and it had belonged to her mother. Anyway, after that fight over the stolen ring, they never saw each other again, and her friend had since died, and then thirty years later here was the ring. She was so sad, almost inconsolable, but finally I told her that her piano was in tune, and ready to be played, and that seemed to brighten her up. She thanked me, and gave me a tip, but I never did tune that piano again.

Pause.

Bob: It was a piano full of regrets.

Bob feels the ring, then tries it on his ring finger…

Bob: You know, I was once married.

Bob pockets the ring, then returns to the piano and carefully feels underneath and behind the piano keys. His search leads him back to the key, where he finds an earring. He feels the earring. It is very cheap and gaudy. He mutters to himself.

Bob: Jesus, junk jewelry, like something you'd find at the fair…

Silence.

Bob decides to stay and work on the derelict piano, and hastily removes the top board, placing it stage left. While he works…

Bob: It's going to take a mighty effort to bring this piano round to harmony. A mighty effort. And I can tell you one thing about this piano — that it is full of howls and pain. Howls and pain. Like I told you, I'd better damn well tune this piano.

Bob sits and begins tuning, but the instrument is recalcitrant.

Bob: Jesus. Jesus Murphy… How d'ya expect me to ever tune this piano?

He discovers a pair of scissors crammed into the wires. He feels them and is stunned by his memory.

Bob: Solingen. Germany. Keeps a fine edge, and some of the finest steel anywhere. I know these scissors…barbering scissors.

He crosses behind the piano stool, holding the scissors. He starts snipping so the sound of the scissors can be heard.

Scene 2: Bob the Barber

Bob: You know, about twenty years, twenty pounds less, and five lifetimes ago, I worked as a barber. I lived in a small prairie town. It was a pretty small town. I cut the hair of the locals. Mostly they were Mormons. You know, the Church of Latter Day Saints. It was a good job. I knew pretty much everybody in town. On the outskirts of the town, there was a military base, and I'd also cut the hair of the military men. I had a wife, and she was beautiful. She had black curly hair, and dark-dark eyes. The first time I laid eyes on her was at the skating rink. Wow, she could move and twist like a dust devil. The second time I laid eyes on her was at the church where she was playing hymns for the Mormons.

Pause. Just the sound of the scissors.

Bob: Her name was Marie.

Pause. Just the sound of scissors.

Bob: We had a baby boy...you know, a cute baby boy. We called him Baby Boy — because, you know, that was the name that stuck.

Pause. Just the sound of scissors.

Music cue: Distant piano playing an old-time tune.

Bob: Marie was a piano teacher. She taught on an old upright that she gave plenty of love and attention. She had big milkmaid's hands but, man, could she play that piano. Marie was the best damn thing to happen to me then and ever since. I was in love with her and many times, many times I told her: "Marie, you and Baby Boy are all I have in the world."

It was a cool day in July, because there was one of those winds that blow across the prairies. Some may call it an ill wind, but it blew. Now that ill wind blows the door open to my barbershop and in walks this tall military man. He is a Captain. Now I ask the Captain to take a seat in my barber chair, and the Captain removes his tall military hat and sits. I work my magic with the scissors.

Pause. Just the sound of scissors.

Bob: The Captain asks me, "Who is playing the piano?" I says, "It's the wife."

Pause.

Music cue: Music fades.

Bob: Just at that moment, Marie comes into the shop to look for her metronome, you know, her metronome, and the Captain's eyes meet hers...those dark-dark eyes. His gaze seems to open up something in her and she explodes in a strange kind of laughter. Laughter?

Pause. Just the sound of the scissors...

Bob: Well, before I know what's happened, I've accidentally cut the ear of the Captain. There's blood all over the scissors, blood all over the Captain. Marie — she has to put on Band-Aids.

Bob backs away in shame, wiping the "blood" off the scissors, then places them on the piano... He turns and addresses the audience.

Bob: You know, I don't know what came over me.

Bob places the scissors on the piano. He sits on the stool and begins to work again, tuning the instrument. A note sounds.

Bob: Here we go. Now we're back in business.

Scene 3: Bob has an Argument with a Piano

Bob: So what is wrong with this instrument? Everything. It's dry, hoarse, dead — it needs, at the very least, new strings and pins, and desperately needs some care and attention, but I can't give any guarantees that it'll ever play in tune.

Bob readjusts a few notes, then addresses the piano directly:

Bob: What comes out of you is just old squeaks and squawks and, believe me, you son of a bitch, you are finished.

Bob struggles with a pin and then accidentally drops his tuning hammer inside the piano. He half climbs into the piano searching for the hammer. The hammer is stuck. Bob mutters as he pulls on the tuning hammer.

Bob: Shit, I know it's you... You can't forgive. You laughed. Everybody knew what was going on...even the Mormons. You two were like flies screwing on the windowsill on a hot day in August. Your laughter was hot-hot, and I couldn't look into those dark-dark eyes anymore.

Bob gives another mighty heave.

Bob: I can't believe that you'd pull a trick like this. Can't you find anything better to do than...to...torment...me!

Bob gives a huge tug, then stumbles downstage with the hammer... He is caught for a moment... He turns to the public and speaks to them.

Bob: Sorry. Sometimes you have to get personal with pianos, and it seems this piano needs personal care and attention...like, real personal...like, how do you do, you crappy old upright?

He thrusts his hand inside the piano and digs around.

Bob: What the — ?

Bob struggles with something, trying to find a string or something that is blocked inside…then he pulls out an old photograph. He feels it with his hands.

Bob: A photograph… Jesus, I'll find out what is jamming up this damned third octave — God, what a mess…

Bob continues to work. He grabs what looks like a small bicycle wheel, pulls it out…and grabs it with both hands.

Bob: *(With irony.)* Jeez, where'd they put the rest of the car?

The wheel has a central pivot, and he begins to turn the wheel…

Music cue: The sound of carnival music and sounds of people screaming on a thrill ride.

Scene 4: Bob and the Talking Horse

Bob: The county fair and rodeo…

Bob crosses downstage, turning the wheel slowly.

Bob: I took the wife and Baby Boy. The night air smelled like horseshit and warm candy floss. A lot of the military men with brush cuts went to the carnival looking for action. I took Marie for a ride on the Ferris wheel and it was wild. The lights, the crowds, booths to play all kinds of games: ring toss, knock down cans, whack-a-gopher, and there was the side show, with all the freaks — the Rubber Man, the Bearded Lady, and the Lobster Boy. The most popular was the Talking Horse, who gave out premonitions on crops, rainfall, and advice on when to plow and seed. You paid fifty cents and the horse would stomp on the ground and talk in a gruff voice. It was fake but supposed to be really funny. Even some of the Mormon farmers snuck in to hear what that horse had to say. Many locals believed in that horse sense.

From the upstage side of the piano a neon sign of the Talking Horse appears. The Talking Horse sounds like a poor imitation of Elvis. Bob crosses stage right with "Marie" and "Baby Boy"...

Bob: I took Marie and Baby Boy to see the Talking Horse, paid fifty cents, and the horse stomped three times then reared its head back and whinnied fearfully. There was a wild look in its eyes. Marie fell back into my arms, and the Horse spoke:

Sound cue: Elvis voice-over.

Voice: "Once upon a time, there was a baby boy who had lost his mother and father. Everything was dead and there was nothing in the whole wide world. And because there was nothing in the whole world, the boy went away and searched day and night. And because there was nothing left on earth, he decided to go to heaven, and the moon looked at him so kindly! But when he reached the moon he found it was a piece of rotting wood. And when he went to the sun, he found it was a withered sunflower, and when he came to the stars, they were golden gnats that a crow had stuck on a blackthorn bush, and when he wanted to go back to the earth, all that was left was a broken piano, and he crawled into the piano, and lived like a wild child...and he cried, and he is still there, all alone..."

Bob: Marie was terrified and bolted from the tent. I stood still for a long time, just staring at that horse...

You know, I don't know what came over me...

Marie ran out of the tent and straight into the arms of the Captain. He was dressed in his civvies, just lookin' for action.

You know, I don't know what came over her...

I ran through the crowds holding on to Baby Boy for dear life. Damn if he didn't lose his little shoe, and I had to go back to look for it.

Damn, I never did find that shoe.

Bob spins the wheel faster.

Bob: I asked some of the military men, and they said they'd seen Marie and the Captain jump on the Ferris wheel. I saw the Captain give Marie something shiny. She told me later that she'd won in them in a game — the little mechanical claw snatched the cheap plastic earrings... The Ferris wheel spun through the warm-horseshit-and-candy-floss-smelling air then into the clear starry night. From hot to cold, and cold to hot. I watched as my beautiful wife was spun away into the night. I was holding on for dear life to our bawling-piss-in-his-diapers-and-one-shoed Baby Boy.

Bob spins the wheel faster and faster until it spins from his hands. He waits until it stops. Bob remembers the gaudy junk earring in his pocket. He hangs onto the earring throughout the rest of the scene, like a talisman of pain.

Bob: It was exactly like that. I never touched her, never did, but scared her with my eyes. You know, that "I'm-gonna-kill-you" look. I saw the two of them wheeling around, from hot to cold, and cold to hot. I knew you two were up to something. Something was up. And it wasn't right.

Bob collects his thoughts. The neon horse vanishes. Bob stumbles around the space, finding his things.

Bob: Is this some kind of practical joke?

Silence.

Bob: I don't know who you are, or why you are doing this to me, but I'll tell you, this is no joke. You phone me, I come all the way down here on the bus, walk through the snow, find my way into this hall, and you have this piece of garbage for me to tune... I can't see it. But feel it, here, and here, and look at these cracks, and graffiti, and rounded-off edges in the case. Maybe there's something beautiful and fragile left here, but I haven't found it. All I can find is dirt and filth and someone else's memories.

Pause.

Bob: You can't fool me. Tell me what you want from this old rotting carcass. Listen, whoever you are, if you want to play, let's find a new piano, or at least one that can be tuned. Do you hear me? Huh? Do you hear me!

Silence.

Bob: Marie!

With disgust and barely contained rage, Bob thrusts the earring into his pocket. He crosses upstage to the piano, picks up the tuning hammer and slashes at the piano wire...

Pause.

Just the sound of Bob breathing.

Bob discovers a single old leather skate inside the wires. He grabs it and holds onto it, then sits on the piano stool.

Music cue: Cheesy skating music that sounds like it's being played on tinny, crackling outdoor speakers can be heard.

Scene 5: Kick and Twirl

Bob: There aren't too many more beautiful things to do in a small town on a winter night than go down to the local rink for a skate. Marie would leave Baby Boy at the barbershop and walk down to the town rink that was built by the Mormons, although they weren't allowed to skate. There was a full moon. Marie's edges were sharp, always sharp, because I would sharpen them with my grinder. Marie could do some of the fancier moves. You know, dig her steel picks into that diamond-hard crystal ice, and shove off...

Bob gets up off the stool, and begins moving the skate.

Bob: ...and kick and twirl, kick and twirl, kick and twirl.

That night the Captain comes down to the rink. He stands against the end boards, watching her wild moves as she kicks into the diamond-hard ice and twirls, then catches a sure edge with her sharp skates.

The Captain catches her eye and waves, and Marie darts towards the Captain at breakneck speed. A few other skaters peel away as she bears down on the boards. Then, on a dime, she twists her weight and covers the Captain in a plume of dry, dry snow and ice particles.

The Captain laughs, Marie laughs — and the Captain says the words:

"Do you wanna drink of whiskey, Marie, as a warmer-upper?"

Bob slams the skate onto the piano stool.

Bob: Dammit. She wanted a warmer-upper!

Bob reels around, thinking he is addressing the perpetrator of this crime...

Scene 6: Bob Continues his Argument with the Piano

Bob: I'm pissed off, I'm telling you. I'm pissed off...this is no piano-tuning, it's some kind of insane and prolonged bad joke. What am I supposed to do, huh?

Pause.

You can forget this game of hide and seek, or show and tell, or whatever you are trying to do to me, because I'm telling you, whatever you did to this piano is sick, sick. I can tell you that if you don't show yourself now...

Silence.

Bob walks directly downstage, breaking the fourth wall, and addressing the audience...

Bob: You know, a blind man has got a sixth sense — knows how many people are in the room and where they are — like a bat has radar. I'm in tune with the room, if you get my meaning.

But I don't sense anything dangerous...

Pause.

Bob: A piano is a lot like us, a bundle of vibrating chords, and a bit of a puzzle, waiting to be caressed, to be loved maybe. A piano can be stubborn, even full of bullshit. But most of all, a piano has a memory — it can remember.

Bob realizes that he might know who is tormenting him. He crosses upstage, creeping up to the piano.

He begins moving his hands very slowly up and down the keys, until his hands stop on the right key.

Suddenly he pounds on a key, then lunges for something in the piano. It's a bottle... He grabs it, and sneers at the piano.

Scene 7: Spin the Bottle

Bob: A-hah! Got ya...I knew it. Spin the Bottle. The Captain and Marie played Spin the Bottle, right in the living room. I went to the military base to give haircuts to the soldiers, and Marie played some drinking songs...

Music cue: Drinking songs on a piano.

Bob: Spin the Bottle; what are the rules, what are the rules? If the bottle points to ya, you gotta take one piece of yer clothes off. Marie banged out all the drinkin' songs she could remember.

Bob kneels in front of the keyboard and starts sniffing around the keys, moving his nose up the keys until he stops...

Bob: It was here; they were like two flies screwing on a windowsill on a hot August day. I can smell it in the keys. It's still there, and I can smell it...

Have you ever smelled a piano?

The music builds to a raunchy crescendo...

Bob: I smell Marie's bare ass bouncing up and down on the keys. It was pretty exciting for the Captain. He discovered that night that Marie had a strawberry birthmark in the shape of three half-notes on the inside of her left thigh...

They banged out tunes in the lower scales, they smacked double-time on the higher octaves, they even played four-hands and two-cheeks.

Pause.

Bob: And the bottle spun and the bottle spun.

It's in the keys; they left their filthy dirty screwing smell in the keys...

Bob crosses stage left, his back towards the piano, humiliated and enraged.

Scene 8: Bob has a Futile Fight with the Piano

Bob: *(Speaking jaggedly.)* Okay, damn you. You are right...what did I think? That this was going to be a twenty-minute job, replace the string while the pianist sweats in the wings, waiting for the tuner to finish his job? This son-of-a-bitch upright will kill me, but it will be a fight to the finish, I'm telling you that...

Bob crosses stage left and challenges the piano to a fight.

Bob: Ladies and gentlemen, please welcome tonight in the ring of impossible harmony: In this corner, me, Bob the Tuner, armed only with his tuning hammer and fine and nimble hearing. Bob is legally blind, but can tune up a grand piano in half a day, and is famous for dependable and reliable tunings.

Versus: In this corner, the rotten, the disgusting, the dirty, the dangerous Mr. Upright, a demon-infested, vermin-infested, cowardly piano that loves to eat and spew garbage and lies, but worse yet, loves to play old trashy tunes. And watch out for his moves in the corner. He knows how to throw his weight around.

Ladies and gentlemen, and I mean all ladies and gentlemen, you know the rules. Never hit below the hammers; watch for hidden and dangerous materials.

Ding… Round one.

Bob leaps at the piano. He struggles, pulling on the fall board, which almost crushes his hands.

Bob: Now, you scum, I will knock your octaves into harmony, and bring this foul-smelling derelict back into tune, if it's the last thing I do…

Bob crosses stage left, then turns to attack the instrument…

Bob: From now on, I will be the boss here. I will tune you or be crushed by you, you son of a bitch, you quarrelsome lying tank of an upright.

Bob crosses downstage, trying to jam his tuning fork into the void inside the piano's "chest," but slips. The piano rocks forward as he falls, but he catches it…

Bob: Aha! The infamous piano-tuner-crushing move. You know you can't forgive, and forget, you are a son of a bitch, bitch, bitch… BITCH!

With a huge effort Bob pushes the piano back to its upright position and then thrusts the tuning hammer into the empty cavity of the derelict piano, stabbing over and over…

The piano keys are rigged with preset drum triggers. As Bob pounds on the keys in various octaves, instead of musical notes, sounds are cued: the sound of a woman screaming, a baby crying, the sounds of an ambulance. All this builds into a high-pitched wail, then a series of decrescendos, all played on an out-of-tune piano…

Bob pulls out his arm from the instrument and looks at his tuning hammer. Then he looks to the audience and drops the tuning hammer, stunned… He falls forward, banging his head on the piano. He is knocked out and collapses downstage. The piano begins to fall on top of Bob…

Blackout:

Video projector cue: During the blackout, an old silent black-and-white Super-8 film is projected on the canvas backdrop hanging upstage. The film shows the hands of a mother and her son playing a piano. Then the mother's hands stop playing, and she grasps the boy's hands in desperation. Then we see pictures of skates, a Ferris wheel, a barbershop, intercut with prairie landscapes and piano keys. Then we see only a small boy's hands playing scales, over and over, and images of sheet music. The hands become skillful and then we begin to hear music, being played expertly with care and attention. The music and the film are speeded up to a hysterical level. The music and images stop abruptly as the lights snap up to a cold brightness… There is a harsh gobo effect of bars projected across the piano.

Sound cue: Prison gates slamming shut.

(Two minutes.)

Part 2

The Piano Full of Shadows and Terror

Scene 9: Step-by-Step Mail Order Program of Piano Tuning

The lights come up quickly. Bob is lying face up with the piano on top of him. Bob bangs on the piano with his hand.

Bob: This is pretty much exactly how it feels to be in prison.

Bob bangs on the piano with his hand.

Bob: You can't move because you have a piano on your chest.

Bob bangs on the piano with his hand.

Bob: There is nothing to do but accept the weight of a piano called justice.

Bob bangs on the piano with his hand.

Bob: There is nothing to learn but accept that you have a piano on your chest, keep your head down, don't mess with the screws, and never tell anyone you have a piano on your chest.

Bob bangs on the piano three times.

Bob: What did I learn in jail?

This prison chaplain asked me, "What about a career as a piano technician and tuner, Bob? Why don't you consider the advantages? It's a rewarding career for a blind man."

Slowly, Bob struggles to push the piano off him... Slowly, the awkward and difficult sounds of a piano being tuned are heard under his words.

Bob: Stress-free work: No deadlines, no time clock or boss. Just the piano and you.

Flexible hours: Full-time or part-time.

Versatility: From piano tuning, you can branch out into other profitable areas such as piano moving, piano refinishing and rebuilding, and buying and selling of pianos.

Low overhead: Many tuners work from their own garages and homes.

Job satisfaction: You will gain a great deal of pleasure from taking old, beat-up, unplayable pianos and turning them into something useful and beautiful.

Honourable profession: You will make a useful, respectful contribution to society.

Ease of training: With our course, you will work at your own pace, in your home, learning step by step how to proceed into this rewarding career.

With a mighty heave, Bob rights the piano.

Is this the kind of work for you? Why not you? So I wrote to the American School of Piano Tuning, and the piano lifted for moments off my chest, and I could finally feel that weight shift and begin to make sense of what all that shit was on top of me.

Bob crosses stage right, finds the stool, crosses centre stage, then sits down…

Bob: Step by step, one step at a time.

In prison, I'll tell you, it's not easy to become a piano tuner. A piano is considered a potential weapon; just consider all those miles of piano wire. But there was a piano in the chapel, and I was escorted three days a week, with two guards. I could enter that chapel, then pull on those strings…

Music cue: Old-time hymn plucked on strings.

Bob: ...on that old piano and the music would waft me past the electric gates, the bars, the dark shadows in other men's thoughts, the fights, the pen and ink tattoos, the shooting galleries, up and over the terrible beauty of the silver razor wire, and console me, waft me into the realm of celestial dreams.

It was a piano...full of shadows.

The music builds in intensity. As the theme progressively builds, Bob's spirit is lifted by the musical piece. Feeling his way, he begins to move around the piano, becoming increasingly confident. Then he climbs on top of the piano. He stands there, his hands raised in an entreating pose, his face held upward, but his eyes tightly closed...

Bob: *(He cries to the heavens.)* Who are you? Where are you? Why am I here?

Silence.

Bob sits on the top of the piano.

Pause.

Bob: In prison, at Christmas, the chaplain would play carols on the newly tuned upright in the chapel — then he'd give out calendars and bags of jelly beans. Sugar, time, music — the perfect gifts.

One Christmas, he arrived with an envelope for me. Inside was an old newspaper clipping. He asked me if he could read it to me — it was a story about a small boy who'd been discovered living inside an old upright piano. When the cops found him, he was playing an old-time hymn on the abandoned old piano.

Pause.

Bob: *(Whispering to himself.)* Baby Boy! Baby Boy!

Bob looks at his hands. They begin to shake.

Bob: Jail — even 24 hours of it — changes you. But I'll tell you something funny. The day I left, the screws told me that the piano in the chapel was dangerously...well, in tune. And the boys would now have to learn to sing Christmas carols in tune...

I'm living proof that the Step-by-Step Mail Order Program of Piano Tuning saved my life.

Bob climbs down warily form the top of the piano.

Bob: Easy there, old upright. Easy. That's it, easy does it.

Scene 10: Bob The Tuner and the Abyss

Bob grabs his cane and whacks the piano. As he circles and bangs the piano, his pace gradually speeds up.

Bob: So what is it you want from me? I fell into an abyss and a piano fell on top of me. I've crawled out and followed the step-by-step program of piano tuning, and spent the past ten years making a respectful and useful contribution to society. I just show up at the appointed hour, tools in hand, and do the job. Nobody, nobody, not until now, has ever cared to ask the blind piano tuner about his past.

Bob turns and walks downstage, breaking the fourth wall, and speaking directly to the audience.

Bob: Or asks me what I can hear that nobody else can. Like a shoe that squeaks, that has a pitch in high C, I can hear that... A door slamming in the third B below middle C, I can hear that... The millions of tiny sounds you all make when you doubt something, I can hear that...

Short breath, I can hear that...

A rustle in your pocket when you pull out the cash to pay me, I can hear that... I can hear your heartbeat increase when you are nervous — I can hear that... The moment just before your fingertips touch a newly tuned instrument, I can hear that... I can hear when you smile, and take my arm and show me to the door... I can hear you just sitting there fingering your programmes, just waiting for the concert to begin.

I can hear that.

Bob speaks to the heavens.

Bob: But why can't I hear you? Why can't I hear you?

Bob rushes back to the piano, and this time he opens it carefully...plays through some of the bass section to check his work...

Bob: Bass section, the beats are corrected nice, good, good. Now the treble section, let's check. E-G-B-D-F — nothing. Again, E-G-B-D-F, E-G-B-D-F. Remember that old beginning piano game? E — Every, G — Good, B — Boy, D — Deserves, F — Fudge.

Bob touches the F key.

Music cue: The sound of a baby crying is heard. Bob reels backward from the piano towards stage left, scared... He takes the stool with him.

Bob: Son of a bitch, this piano is at it again. What in God's name do you want? Jesus, don't tell me there is more garbage in this piano, 'cause I don't want to know. I told you, I don't know what came over me.

Okay, Marie, maybe we shouldn'ta listened to that goddamned Talking Horse! Now show yourself, the game is over. Marie, Marie. Marie, I can't bring you back, all that black hair, and the way you kicked that diamond-hard ice with your picks and twirled.

Bob spins wildly on the piano stool.

Bob: I would count out the seconds before you landed, your scarf twisting around in the wind before the sharp blade caught the ice again…

Bob is thrown stage left by the momentum of the spinning stool. As he stops, the piano explodes with the notes E-G-B-D-F over and over. Bob rushes to listen to the keys move all by themselves…

Bob: Okay…E-G-B-D-F, Every Good Boy Deserves Fudge.

The piano sounds the F again.

Bob: Favours…

The piano sounds the F again.

Bob: Fries…

The piano sounds the F again.

Bob: Food…

The piano sounds the F again.

Bob: Every Good Boy Deserves… Son of a bitch, I don't know… Father. Every Good Boy Deserves Father. Father. Father.

All the notes are played, then a piece of "Chopsticks."

Bob backs away from the piano warily. He listens to the notes and then approaches the piano from a new angle, certain he'll find something. The piano continues to play on its own… He listens…

Bob: E-G-B-D-F. But then there is a progression. It doesn't end at F…A…

It continues up the scale, E-G-B-D-F…A…C…E-G-B-D-F-A-C-E? A-C-E? What about F…A…C…E? F-A-C-E. F-A-C-E…

Face. Face.

Sound and music cue: A huge crack of thunder, foreboding music. Bob cowers. Then he slowly turns the piano around. As he turns the piano, two large doors on the back of it open.

His voice trembles.

Bob: It's time to face the music…

I can hear the ill wind. I know what's inside there…

I know what you want…

The piano full of terror.

Bob spins the piano around. He opens two large doors on the back of the piano to reveal a painted triptych, comprising the two doors and a wooden panel on the back of the piano. The painting is of a piano and a blood-red moon. In this scene are two puppet heads, a male (Bob) and a female (Marie). The Bob puppet holds a barbering razor. The Marie puppet has one gaudy earring.

Scene 11: Bob Faces The Music

A spotlight catches Bob's face. He crosses behind the piano, and then steps up and kneels to manipulate the puppets. Bob says the lines for the two puppets.

Sound cue: The wind and voices increase in volume during the scene.

Puppet B: Marie, you're home late from skating. Baby Boy was crying.

Puppet M: He'll be okay. I'll play him a lullaby.

Puppet B: Marie, you have whiskey breath.

Puppet M: I had a warmer-upper.

Puppet B: Yeah, a warmer-upper.

I see you still got those earrings…

Puppet M: It's a little joy I have.

Bob, don't you dare look at me with those eyes.

Puppet B: What eyes, Marie?

Marie, look at the moon. Just go look at the moon.

Puppet M: It's the colour of iron.

Puppet B: Remember the Talking Horse, Marie?

Puppet M: What are you saying, Bob?

Puppet B: It's nothing, Marie. I'm cold, Marie.

I saw you screwing like two drunken flies on a windowsill on a hot day in August. Your dirty and filthy smell was on the cold piano keys.

Puppet M: Hot, cold, cold hot. Make up your mind, Bob. What is in your hand?

Puppet B: Just my barbering razor.

Puppet M: What are you doing, Bob? Wait, Bob. Bob. Stop, Bob. Stop, Bob.

Sound cue: A woman screams.

Bob cries to the heavens... He takes the barbering razor from puppet Bob's hand.

Bob: Marie, Marie...you and Baby Boy are all I had in the world!

Bob removes his dark glasses and slashes his eyes. He writhes in pain, then collapses, tortured and tragic.

Pause.

Bob: Silence, a moment of silence. For Marie. Silence!

Silence for one complete minute.

At the end of the minute of silence, Bob slowly climbs off the piano, closes the doors, and pivots the piano back to its original position. As he does, a bronzed baby shoe is seen on the fall board of the piano...visible to everyone except Bob. He takes a couple of steps towards the public, trying to feel the mood in the house...

PART 3

THE PIANO FULL OF MIRACLES

Scene 12: The Piano Full of Miracles

Bob: *(With a quiet finality.)* We all have to look into the abyss. And yeah, some us fall right in, and nothing — and I mean nothing — happens until we hit bottom.

And if I had all the power in the world, I'd rewrite that moment. Do you hear me? I'd rewrite that moment, because I know I have at least a million other scenarios that I'd prefer.

Bob collapses to his knees, pleading.

Bob: I don't know what came over me.

Quietly and directly to audience.

Bob: Rage, jealousy, anger, shame...the list is as long as my arm...

Bob: You know, being blind isn't always about loss of sight...

Bob crosses to find the top board stage left. He sets it back into position.

But hey, you know all about this. It was you who set the trap, drew me in, till this piano and tuner spilled their guts. Listen, whoever you are, this piano is ready. It's cleaned out, the strings are primed tight. It's got its voice back. The hammers are ready to strike the coiled alloy wires. The tension in a piano is something to behold. Nineteen tons — enough to hang two city buses right here in this hall. So what is it? What is it that you want me to say?

Bob: *(With ironic sang-froid.)* Hang the piano tuner?

Bob: *(With remorse.)* I'm sorry, Marie.

Silence.

Bob: I'll tell you what I know.

The tuner exits before the concert. There is no applause for a well-tuned piano. It just is. There is harmony. It's only noticed when that chord is unstrung, and then everything goes to hell in a handbasket.

So I'm making my exit.

Bob is about to leave. He finds his white cane and tuning hammer. He lets his hand slide down the fall board and his hand discovers the bronzed baby shoe. He is overcome by the memories. He staggers back, stunned.

From stage right beaming lights strafe the stage. Bob senses the lights and turns to face them.

Bob: Baby Boy, Baby Boy, Baby Boy! Is it you? This is your baby shoe…and here you are. Is it you? Well, tell me, what do you look like? Jesus, Jesus, I don't know what to say… Say something, 'cause I'm just standin' here all alone…wait, wait, wait… You did this, Baby Boy?

Say something, 'cause I need to hear you.

Baby Boy… Dammit, I've brought this piano back from the dead… It's got life in it. It is a piano full of miracles… Listen… Listen…

Bob plays a few notes on the piano. The notes ring true.

Bob: Remember that Talking Horse? I was holding you in my arms — maybe that was the last time — and I held you like that. I'll never forget it. You lost this shoe…

Once upon a time, there was a baby boy who lost his father and mother. Everything was dead, and there was nothing left in the whole wide world. Everything was dead and he went away and searched day and night. And because there was nobody left on earth he thought he would go up to heaven, and the moon looked at him so kindly! But when he reached the moon he found it was a piece of rotting wood. And when he went to the sun, he found it was a withered sunflower, and when he came to the stars, they were golden gnats that a crow had stuck on a blackthorn, and when he wanted to go back to earth, the earth was a broken piano.

Bob cradles the little bronzed shoe in his hands. His hands are shaking.

Bob: Baby Boy.

A recorded voice-over in a younger man's voice takes over.

Voice: ...And the baby boy lived in that piano like a wild child until he was taken away and he was raised by kind people. He searched day and night until he found the derelict piano, long ago abandoned and forgotten. He prepared it with memories so terrible and violent, but knew that one day, with memories and music, he would find his father...

Bob grabs his cane.

Bob: Lost and found, terrible, violent.

Abandoned, forgotten.

Those words cut us all like razors...

Okay, Baby Boy, Baby Boy, I'm making my exit.

Pause.

Bob touches the piano lovingly and starts to walk toward the strong light stage right.

Bob: The piano is ready. It's got some of its harmony back… Go ahead, son…play the music.

Bob exits into the light, and raises his arms… Music begins to play. Then the huge beam of sidelight fades slowly, leaving the piano in a wash of backlight.

Blackout.

FIN

Afterword

In 1995, in a little diner on the Alaska Highway on the outskirts of Whitehorse, Yukon, I had a chance meeting with Zubin Gillespie, an itinerant piano tuner and traveller. I was curious about his work and he began telling me some of his odd and wonderful stories about piano tuning and travel. He even invited me along to listen and watch as he tuned a piano. As I watched him bring the instrument into tune, I marvelled at the painstaking and precise work, the extraordinary physical positioning, the dexterity, and the absolute knowledge of the instrument required for the job, not to mention the willingness to tackle an instrument that is holding literally thousands of pounds of tension. I imagine that individuals who want to work alone at this time-honoured craft are a rarity. Since the machinery of the acoustic piano has not changed radically in three hundred years, these tuners can pretty much work on anything. It was fascinating to watch him and listen to him work. His devotion to the craft inspired me to write about these workers who come into our homes and bring pianos back to tune.

Because I am a storyteller by nature, thoughts and questions started coming to me: What if an old piano was a repository of stories? What were the stories held within the coiled strings that could be released only by a piano tuner? I also began to wonder about the memories of the piano tuner. And how could I fuse these thoughts together?

I began working on a narrative poem about a young piano tuner who finds a military man lying in a pool of blood on the keyboard of an derelict old upright. The piano is haunted by this story. Then the piano is shipped by various owners to different locales — a townhouse in Baltimore, the jungles of Vietnam, and finally an old log house somewhere in the wilderness of Nova Scotia. The poem was theatrical, perhaps even cinematic. I wasn't really thinking of it as a performance piece, until the composer Daniel Janke asked me to take part in his music- and story-driven "Longest Night Festival" at the Yukon Arts Centre in Whitehorse the following year, in 1996. I reduced the poem to about fifteen minutes and Daniel wrote music to support the short performance.

The evening went well. I liked the character and the music interaction, but the story didn't have enough drive and presence — it all took place in the past tense and it really wasn't immediate enough for a one-man show. Plus, I was in the middle of writing *The Hats of Mr. Zenobe*. I shelved the idea with the hope that I might use the character again in a play.

In September 1997 I experienced one of the darkest periods of my life. At the time, I didn't think I would ever write or perform again. By the time the ordeal came to an end, I understood tragedy — mentally, emotionally and physically. It was in my bones. I knew that I would never be able to write again without that tragedy being a presence.

In November 1998, I moved out of the Yukon to make a new life. I moved to Montreal like a refugee — with nothing except two suitcases. In one of the suitcases was a draft of the piano tuner poem. Once I had set up my life, I read the poem again and I knew that this was the story I needed to tell. And I knew it would have to be a tragedy.

I began by contacting piano tuners and interviewing them, asking them questions about their work and asking them to share any unusual stories or jokes. They all seemed to be very decent men who loved their jobs, loved working alone and, of course, loved pianos. The one thing they seemed to have in common was that they had plenty of opinions about everything. I came to believe that the "Zen" of piano tuning — the combination of deep listening and working alone — can lead the mind to extraordinary conclusions. At least that is my conclusion about piano tuners.

From the piano tuners I also heard many stories about finding objects in pianos — keys, rings, mice, cat food. One tuner in New York City even told me about finding a rolled-up wad of Civil War-era hundred-dollar bills. The tuners were forthcoming and sometimes even a little embarrassed to recount their stories that were fuelled with a quirky charm and offbeat humour. Another aspect of the profession that interested me was that blind men were often perfect candidates for the job. The Canadian National Institute for the Blind (CNIB) used to train men and later women to tune pianos. My family had a piano, and I have a strong memory of the blind tuner working on the family instrument.

A large part of this initial research for the play was to find a piano that would be the central object. Pianos are beautiful, but can also be very boring to look at on stage. I was really seeking a derelict with character. I scoured the want ads and searched in various piano shops. Finally, at Montreal Piano in the Plateau district in Montreal, a wonderful old piano restoring and repair shop run by a Croatian family, I discovered the central object I wanted for the show, an 1899 Schumann Brothers upright grand piano. It was in appalling condition, covered with carved initials and graffiti and over-painted with brown and beige paint; it was obvious that the poor instrument had sat for years in some school auditorium or church basement before being sent to the boneyard. That was the defining moment for the new attack on this piece. I had found the central object. With this piano in mind, I went to work on writing various drafts. Thanks to a Canada Council for the Arts writing grant, I was able to focus my time and thoughts on the new piece. In the spring of 2002, I travelled to Brussels to the flea market to search for more objects — and returned with some brilliant pieces — old piano tuner's tools, a pair of old leather skates and a bronzed baby shoe.

Through this search for the central idea, I realized the tragic hero would be a blind piano tuner — and it would be his story. It would have the central theme of a man who falls into the abyss, but finds redemption. In preparation I reread another tragedy that featured a man who falls into the abyss, Georg Büchner's *Woyzeck* (Victor Price's English translation of the original *Woyzeck,* published by Oxford University Press, 1971). I was shocked by his uncompromising honesty, and vivid short sharp scenes of Soldier Woyzeck's falling into a trajectory of tragedy. That gave me the idea of a man, blind to his emotions, who is overcome by jealousy and murders his beloved wife. The story of the tragic fall of an ordinary man resonated with me and Woyzeck's story was certainly an inspiration. In *The Piano Tuner*, the talking horse monologue is adapted from the English translation of the original Woyzeck[1].

Another inspiration was a wonderful painting by the Canadian artist William Kurelek called "Where Am I? Who Am I? Why Am I?" The central image is a man in a prairie windstorm. He is facing the wind, his face tipped up and his eyes closed. The stark, sad simplicity of the painting made a deep impression on me and memories of visits to southern Alberta came flooding back. I thought that perhaps now that I had some distance from the prairies, I could actually write another prairie play, the first one since I co-created *One Beautiful Evening* with Small Change Theatre for Edmonton's first Fringe Theatre Festival in 1982.

From the very outset of this project, when Daniel Janke set the long poem version to music, I felt that an original score and sound design were absolutely necessary for this creation. In all my applications seeking development and writing money I asked for a composer to work with me. I knew that sound and music were closely linked to the narrative and I understood the emotional qualities I was looking for. In the spring of 2001 I was commissioned by the CBC to adapt *Heart of a Dog* into a one-hour radio drama. For the radio adaptation I wanted a theremin player and composer, and I was lucky enough to find Henry Kucharzyk. He gave me some wonderful ideas to begin writing the new draft, and thoughts about the relationship of tuners and pianos. In the spring of 2002 I asked Henry to compose an original sound and music score for *The Piano Tuner.*

Now I had a rich pool of images and a central story — a blind piano tuner retunes a derelict instrument that has been "prepared" with key objects that reveal the tragedy of the piano tuner's past. The only piece of information that was still missing was who had prepared the piano and why.

During this writing period, as part of my rebuilding my life, I started to do some research to find my biological parents. In April 2002, I received the most incredible letter from my mother. It shook me deeply and I knew this huge fact would affect the piece of writing I was currently working on. On my adoption papers, I was called simply Baby Boy. The deeply personal and hidden story began to emerge from the fog of memory, and I began to weave the story of Baby Boy into *The Piano Tuner*. It is Baby Boy who prepares the piano with objects and stories and then summons the blind piano tuner to a hall somewhere in Southern Alberta. Then in October 2003 more astonishing news arrived: details on my biological father, along with a photo of him. The news wasn't entirely happy, however. My father was not alive; he had taken his own life in 1982.

With all of this new narrative, visual and musical fuel, I set to work. I found a studio in Old Montreal and moved in the piano and some of my gear. Gordon McCall, the artistic director of the Centaur Theatre and Wildside Festival, had invited me to give the premiere performance at the Wildside Festival in January 2003. I finally had everything in place — a studio, and six months of time to work on writing the script and building all the necessary elements into the piano. I also had put together a terrific team of creative artists — Paul Lefebvre, Henry Kucharzyk, Almüt Ellinghaus-Mirbt, Marina Popova, Mindy Parfitt, and David Gow, amongst others. I worked on writing the draft with the help of Paul Lefebvre, and began working with the composer, Henry Kucharzyk, who helped design the trigger system and computer configuration to make the magic happen inside the old upright.

By November 2003, I was ready to invite some friends into the studio to see what I was cooking up. The reading went well, but it certainly didn't have the juice and presence of a major-chord tragedy. I was skirting the topic perhaps, and like many theatre pieces in their infancy, my piece needed an engine. My colleague Paul Lefebvre zeroed in on the problems: I had backed off the tragedy and I had lost the present tense. For any theatre writer, this is a lesson that has to be learned and relearned. During the next few drafts, inspired by a local mover and raconteur, I found the character of Bob the Tuner. That was the major shift the piece needed, and in November and December, with a new draft in hand, I moved out of the studio and into a temporary rehearsal hall at the Geordie Theatre and put the work up on its feet.

I worked with a former student of mine, Mindy Parfitt, who is an immensely talented director, to help me find all the details of performance. In the process I discovered that to really find the blind man and piano tuner, I had to work with my eyes tightly closed and sunglasses on as the "mask."This gave me the authenticity I was seeking to bring a tragic physicality to the character and the specificity that I needed as an actor. I've carried this technique into the performance stage as well, although performing blind has resulted in a few "face plants" into the side of the piano!

In early January 2003, the entire team assembled for the final weeks of preparation for all technical, artistic and creative aspects. It was a terrific and difficult week, but the story, the long story of *The Piano Tuner* was coming to a culmination. It opened January 9, 2003. From a chance cup of coffee meeting with an itinerant piano tuner in the far north of Canada in 1995, to Montreal's Centaur Theatre in 2003, it was a story that became an outrageous dialogue between a blind piano tuner and a prepared piano.

Technical Notes

The Prepared Piano

In keeping with the piano mechanics, we kept all the original doors on the upright, fall board, kickboard, and top door, giving all the access we needed to make the installation.

The upright piano was completely gutted except for the piano keys, which left a cavity above and below the keyboard. All the keys were restrung with elastic bands so the piano keys had life. The piano was restrung with old piano wire, and the pin bed was replaced to give the look and feel of the guts of an old piano. At the back of the piano, two large doors were built to enclose the puppet scene. The puppets are operated from above with a simple wire, and most important is that the razor that the Bob puppet holds is removable. These puppets were highly stylized heads and torsos designed and installed by Almüt Ellinghaus-Mirbt.

The Objects

Pre-set inside the prepared piano are the essential objects for the play: a wedding ring and a gaudy, junk jewelry earring are hidden in the keys; a pair of barber's scissors, an old black and white photograph, a small bicycle wheel, an old skate, and a bottle are all jammed into the strings; and a bronzed baby shoe is placed on the fall board later in the play.

The Sound

The magical operation of the piano keys for the E-G-B-D-F scene, the piano movement, and the placing of the bronzed baby shoe on the piano at the end of the play were done by an on-stage "piano wrangler."

For the sound requirements, a speaker and amplifier were wired into the bottom of the upright. Five electronic drum triggers were set underneath the keys. These triggers were relayed to a drum trigger "brain" built into the bottom of the piano and then relayed via a midi cable to a computer in the booth. When Bob hits the keys at the end of the first half of the play, the triggers are preset with various sounds: a woman screaming, a baby crying and an ambulance siren. The sound operator adjusted the triggers for the second half of the play. A small snake containing AC, speaker wire, and computer cable ran from the back of the piano to various locations.

A full lighting, sound and visual technical description is available from the website: www.voxmiraculous.com

The video is projected onto the upstage wall above the piano on a simple white canvas. Duration of the video is two minutes.

Total duration of the play is 71 minutes.

The Republic of Dreams

The Piano Tuner is the final play in a trilogy I've been working on since 1989. But before talking about this play — both the work and the creative process that led to it — a little background information might be useful. Since 1978 I have been working professionally as an artist. After a year of theatre training in Canada, I was accepted at École Jacques Lecoq, where I went to study in 1977 and 1978. After returning to Canada, I went to Vancouver, where I spent one season touring throughout British Columbia with Axis Mime Theatre. I met Brian Paisley, who was just starting a new company in Edmonton called Chinook Theatre and invited me to join him. In 1980 I returned to Alberta. While I was at Chinook I also began a wonderful and fruitful collaboration with Jan Henderson, Jan Miller and Frank C. Turner. We created Small Change Theatre and produced a mask play called *One Beautiful Evening* for the first-ever Edmonton Fringe Festival. After the festival we decided to continue on together. Small Change Theatre specialized in clown and mask performance style, and we managed the company as a kind of collective — sharing administration, management, tour organizing and fundraising. Over a period of almost ten years we were invited to perform our plays all over the world — including Australia, Singapore, New Zealand, Japan, Great Britain, France, the United States and, of course, Canada.

We had been very successful with the creation and touring of these mostly non-verbal shows, but I felt that there was something missing. Although I didn't feel I could complain — after all, what artist doesn't want to receive invitations to perform from around the world? — I wasn't happy. It was time for a change. It was time for me to leave the company and create and write my own plays. It dawned on me that what was missing for me was language. I wanted to tell a story that was text-based. I knew I would have to let go of the collective idea and work independently as a solo artist.

It was a pretty scary thought. As a company, we had created a world-class repertoire and our agent had told us that our shows were so successful we would be performing them well into our sixties!

That was an even scarier proposition to me, so I began looking for material that would appeal to my new sense of mission. While we were touring in Australia in the spring of 1988, I went off to see a movie on one of our rare nights off. It was a tender, sweet, honest film called *My Life as a Dog* by the Swedish director Lasse Hallestrom. It really stuck with me, and quite out of the blue I remembered a comment that my teacher, the late Jacques Lecoq, had made about my work in a class exercise. He'd said I had the energy and persistence of a Scottish terrier. I was taken with the idea that perhaps I should find a piece of work that was about a dog, or from the point of view of a dog. Explore my "inner dog," you could say. I was also a huge fan of Gary Larsen, the American cartoonist; his dog cartoons in particular had always struck me as hilarious. I became obsessed with finding dog stories and especially dog humour books — you name it, if it had dog humour, I read it. I even came across an odd book written by an eccentric vicar in England who would record his mysterious and secret life as a dog whenever he tippled his port. It was pretty funny stuff, although the poor vicar must have had to consume a huge amount of alcohol.

Later that same year, once we'd returned from another tour of England and Scotland, and not long after I had begun obsessing about dog stories, I went to Montreal to visit my Russian friends, Marina Popova and Alex Nadezdhin. I mentioned that I wanted to create a piece based on a dog's view of the world, and that I was looking for the perfect story. They looked at me with dismay and almost as one said that I had to read Mikhail Bulgakov's novella *Heart of a Dog*. I promised them that if I could find a translated copy I'd read it. On my return to Edmonton I unearthed a copy at a local bookstore. From the moment I read the first couple of paragraphs, the hair on the back of my neck stood up on end. I was completely captivated by Bulgakov's writing. The novella was laced with black humour, the central character was a brilliant fit, and the story was exceptional.

Bulgakov's story is about a starving little mongrel who is taken off the streets of Moscow, fattened up, then used in a radical medical experiment: the pituitary gland and testicles of a recently deceased petty criminal (and part-time balalaika player) are transplanted into the dog. Over a period of weeks a bizarre transformation takes place and the dog "morphs" into a human, albeit with the heart of a dog. The dog-man calls himself Polygraph Polygraphovich Sharikov, a pretty bourgeois handle considering that just a few weeks before he had been a stray mutt mooching for sausage meat on the streets of Moscow.

Following my discovery of Bulgakov and his excoriatingly funny text, I contacted Agnès Limbos, a Belgian actor and performer whose work I admired, and asked her if she would work with me on my solo piece, *Heart of a Dog*. She agreed. I secured funding from the Canada Council and within a year I was in residence in the hamlet of Da Hoek on the outskirts of Brussels, working in Agnès' studio, howling like a Russian dog. We worked on the script over a period of seven months, eight hours a day, five days a week. While we were working on *Heart of a Dog*, I also made my first foray into the old flea market in Brussels, looking for objects that would inspire my writing as well as illustrate some of the stories with imagery rather than text. This was my first introduction to the Brussels flea market and ever since it has become an essential beginning point for my writing and creative process.

Heart of a Dog was the first in my trilogy of one-man "found object theatre" performance pieces. The words *object* and *theatre* are not usually found in the same sentence, and as a style of theatre it tends to be placed in the world of puppet theatre and figure theatre — more out on the fringe than the mainstream and text-based "psychological" theatre.

For me, found objects are the actual evidence or bits of our humanity that have been discarded. Humans are natural collectors. In a lifetime each of us will collect, archive and hoard mountains of objects and name them as keepsakes, mementos, curios, souvenirs, talismans, touchstones, or *objets d'art*. The importance of these objects varies from person to person, but it is artists who sort, recycle and reconfigure objects that inspire scenes, stories, dream sequences, nightmares, keeping a conscious eye on the contemporary, the universal and the personal. Visual artists are particularly keen at this, although in the past few years many crossover artists have established a reputation in contemporary theatre.

Without getting into too much definition and categorization, my personal experience in creating found-object theatre is that during the writing process, the objects — bric-à-brac, family heirlooms, garbage and personal items — inspire the writing and creation. The stories need the objects and the objects need the stories. The objects may or may not come from the same family — plastic dolls vs. bricks, for example — but when objects are introduced as a performance style, the intensity of the audience's participation is increased. Consider what happens when an actor puts on a mask. Something is triggered deep within us. Curiosity, respect for tradition, even repulsion — the mask demands something of us. The same phenomenon occurs with objects. A trigger of curiosity and wonderment is set off. It is then up to the writer/performer to organize these objects into comical or even tragic events, to pull the objects into a coherent story.

I am a gleaner and a bricoleur, always searching for the perfect object that will unlock a story that has been forgotten, left behind and abandoned. What attracts me to these objects? This place? What has led me to these stories? I think I have always been drawn to the hidden or abandoned stories that real objects contain. I was adopted as an infant and never really knew my own story. As an artist I believe I became viscerally attracted to hidden stories, and I believe that an object has a certain resonance, certain hidden truths, that can be unlocked. I look for stories that give the underdog a voice, the lunatic fringe a hearing, the eccentrics and the dispossessed centre stage in the spotlight. I am looking for tales that are inspired by found objects. The characters and stories I create are outrageous, teetering between the hilarious and the tragic. I am always looking for that precarious edge of tragedy and comedy, always attempting to illuminate something that is profoundly human. I want the audience to leave the theatre after a performance with a little flame of hope.

The theatre is a place for magic to happen, and for me objects are the open door into a world of enchantment. Where do I find these objects? Many places, although I've found many of my best objects in a flea market in Brussels, Belgium. The cobblestoned market is like a tiny postage-stamp country in the middle of Brussels. It is a place I call my *Republic of Dreams*.

The Place Jeux des Balles flea market is a remarkable environment — each morning starting about 6:00 a.m., trucks, vans and beat-up old cars pull into the Place Jeux des Balles, and the vendors scramble to stake out their sales territory. Carpets are placed on the cobblestone square and this "buys" the territory. At about 7:00 a.m. the "early birds" come to wander and pick through the piles. Most of the vendors are Arabs, Russians, Czechs, Romanians, Armenians, Albanians and other former eastern Europeans who have found just enough cash to either buy or "obtain" just about everything you can imagine. The local gendarmes often make a sweep in the mornings looking for known thieves, but it's mostly to show the flag. For me, it is a magic place, full of heirlooms, bric-à-brac, junk, toys, lace, entire kitchens, the odd "antique" and even real treasures.

Since 1989, I've made frequent pilgramages to the Place Jeux des Balles to find the essential objects that inspire my writing. In 1996, I returned and found many key objects for my second play in the trilogy, *The Hats of Mr. Zenobe*. The play is based on an Armenian, Vahan Poladian. Poladian was an eccentric with a wonderfully naïve mission — he hoped to change the world with laughter. Like me, Poladian would spend his mornings scavenging through the markets and junk shops. From the assortment of hats, pipes, canes, baubles and bric-à-brac he would build a phantasmagoria of costumes, and then go on a one-man street parade through his village in the south of France. Poladian was an artist — making a selection, using memory, reflection and construction, and then finding a willing audience, which is no different than any so-called "professional artist."

In May 2002, I returned to Brussels and found to my delight that Place Jeux des Balles was still one of the authentic places remaining in Europe to find objects. Happily, the economy of the flea market had remained the same — it was still a place for the marginal and the recently arrived to find essentials, for treasure hunters like myself, and of course for tourists who were looking for that perfect little curio. It was still the ultimate daily garage sale. The prices were cheap — virtually next to nothing compared with the prices in the antique stores and *brocante* stores that lined the nearby streets. The only thing that had changed was the currency. The vendors, who generally have heavy Arabic accents, no longer called "Un franc, un franc." It was now "Un euro, un euro." But the new European currency had done nothing to change the age-old market. It was still like a living Breughel painting — a riot of colours and stuff — with anything and everything for sale, including the kitchen sink.

When I walk through this astonishing little square, it is like wandering through stories made from objects — I see the collections, the personal obsessions, the accumulations of other lives. Hundreds of little narratives form in my mind as I roam the stalls. I am, of course, aware that I am on a different mission than most marketers, who are probably living below the poverty line and need their essentials, mostly pots and pans, but they also seek little treasures for pleasure.

My process of finding objects is a kind of heightened intuitive reality — the objects often seem to jump into my line of vision, so I am not sure if I find them or they find me. At the risk of sounding bizarre, I have to say that it's a very meditative and a quiet Zenlike state. The key is quiet contemplation in the midst of the chaotic noise and "competition" in the market.

Packing my found objects for home is always nerve-wracking, especially in these days of high security. But it's impossible to predict what will be problematic at the security gate: when I declared a broken handgun for *Heart of a Dog*, the customs inspector had no interest in seeing it, but when I declared a plastic potty duck for *The Hats of Mr. Zenobe*, everyone wanted to see it. I was surprised that I even had to declare the potty duck; apparently it was necessary because the potty had been manufactured in the former East Germany. At least, that's what they told me... But maybe it was just that they couldn't really believe that anybody would want to bring a plastic potty duck into Canada. When I arrive home and unpack my treasures in my studio they always seem wonderfully strange and out of context, but they are the beginning of a new play.

For *The Piano Tuner* I began collecting objects and story ideas in 1996. In four days of searching through Place Jeux des Balles, I found a great collection: toy pianos, piano tuner's tools, an incredible pair of old leather skates, an exotic Arabian oil lamp that looked like a little bronze version of Pinocchio and a bronzed baby shoe. This strange combination of found objects would all become woven into the story. They all would become part of my visual archive for this show. The real centrepiece for *The Piano Tuner,* however, was the derelict carcass of a Schumann and Sons upright piano I found in Montreal. Once the shape of the piece had formed, many of the found objects would be installed into the piano.

So how does this quest for found objects become theatre? First I improvise various stories, and then write the stories "up on my feet," in a kind of trial-and-error process, winnowing the chaff from the wheat. Once I find the stories I want to tell, I look for structure and character, and the writing begins.

The inspiration for stories and characters has evolved over the twelve or so years it has taken me create this trilogy. *Heart of a Dog* was inspired by an existing novella, while *The Hats of Mr. Zenobe* was inspired by the story of a real Armenian refugee, Vahan Poladian. For *The Piano Tuner*, I returned home in a sense — to the prairies and a character named Bob. I begin with an idea, an object, a newspaper clipping, a painting, or a chance meeting with an itinerant piano tuner.

During the creation process I often invite other artists to come into my studio and see various chunks of the work-in-progress. These *enchaînements* are meant to keep the work focused and keep the play on the rails. I also work intensely with other collaborator/authors. First I work alone preparing ideas and scenes, then my collaborator-director comes to the studio from time to time to comment on the work and writing. After several months we are ready for the public previews, then the premiere.

Creating this trilogy has been truly an adventure. Working with the many creative artist collaborators in Canada, Belgium and the United States has been at times difficult, at times thrilling. The various collaborators have had an enormous impact on my creative life through the creation of all these works and I would like to thank them all. The list below is the credits for *The Republic of Dreams* trilogy.

Heart of a Dog. Creation 1989 Canada/ Belgium

Agnès Limbos, Didier Caffonnette, Marina Popova, Alex Nadezdhin, Mirra Ginsburg, Françoise Bloch, Marie-Katelin Rutten, Billy Merwick, Daniel Meillieur, Jan Stirling, Michelle Zenon, Carine Ermins, Marc Elst, Daniel Daniel, Luc d'Haegleer, Small Change Theatre, Brian Paisley, Chinook Theatre, Fringe Theatre Festival.

The Hats of Mr. Zenobe. Creation 1997 Canada/ United States

Agnès Limbos, Jim Jackson, Vahan Poladian, Ben Henderson, Bob Hamilton, Annie Avery, Phillip Adams, Alyx Jones, Bev Oliwa, Georgina Brown, Trish Barclay, Smokebrush Arts Centre, Nakai Theatre, Theatre Network, Marina Popova, Hrant Alianak.

The Piano Tuner. Creation 2003 Canada/Quebec

Paul Lefebvre, Henry Kucharzyk, Mindy Parfitt, Almüt Ellinghaus-Mirbt, David Gow, Michael Brunet, Rachel Johnstone, Marina Popova, Pierro Hirsch, Maria Antonella Pelizzari, Gordon McCall, Centaur Theatre, Wildside Festival.

I would also like to thank the various funding bodies who financially supported these creations: The Canada Council for the Arts, The Alberta Foundation for the Arts, The Yukon Government, Commissariat general aux Relations internationals de la Communaute francaise de Belgique. I'd also like to thank Karen Haughian, editor of Nuage Editions, now called Signature Editions, who felt that these works should be published and gave me great encouragement as a playwright and performer to bring these works to wider audiences through the print media. I'd also like to acknowledge the many other artists, stage managers, tour managers, agents and artistic directors who felt that this form of theatre, and these particular stories performed with found objects and solo performance, were important enough to showcase for their audiences.